EDITOR
JESSICA FISHER

DESIGNER
MICHAEL WALTERS

WRITER & ASSISTANT EDITOR
MARCO GENTILE

EDITORIAL CONSULTANT
SPIRO ALAFASSOS

TECHNICAL SUPPORT
LAURA CARTER

SPECIAL THANKS TO BOB AMES, SUZANNE MARCHETTI, MICHAEL OETTEL, MONICA PENCE,
CHUCK THOMPSON, VI RIPKEN, AND MORTON TADDER

PRINTING AND PREPRESS BY FRENCH BRAY GLEN BURNIE, MD

PUBLISHED IN BALTIMORE, MARYLAND

MANUFACTURED IN THE UNITED STATES OF AMERICA.

RIPKEN FAMILY PHOTOGRAPHS CONTAINED ON PAGES:
6,7,8,9,10,12,13,14,15

© 2001 RICH PILLING/ MAJOR LEAGUE BASEBALL PHOTOS
4,18,19,23,25,27,30,38,48,50,62,64,67,68,79,80,81,83 85,89,91,94,95,96,99

PRINCIPLE PHOTOGRAPHY
JERRY WACHTER

foreword

I've tried to think back to the first time I had an inkling that this young kid – Cal Ripken, Jr. – could be special. Well, to be honest, I didn't. I knew he was a big, strong athlete but I had no idea of what kind of a head he had.

I would soon find out, like so many others, that the Ripken family cultivated strong individuals with keen minds and athletic prowess.

When you sat down with Cal Ripken, Sr., you talked baseball. He would inquire about your wife, or if he knew that one of your kids was sick he would ask about it. Otherwise, the topic was baseball. It sounds as if that was all he talked about, but that's not true. The Ripkens have always had the ability to handle family matters and separate them from the ballpark. That's kind of tough, but they've always been able to do it.

There is a time for playing cards and having fun and being with the family. Then, there is a certain time of the day, for people like the Ripkens, when the clock ticks and says "Hey, go to work. Tonight you gotta fight." I think all of the pros are like that.

Being a professional is about work, dedication, concentration, and fine tuning yourself into a well-crafted athlete. If you're a good teacher, you pass those things on. Growing up, you would see Cal, Jr. at the ballpark occasionally, but not that often. Senior was going to work. It was not a place for kids to play. However, he made them well aware of the lessons to be learned on the field. Cal, Sr., Vi and the kids worked together and played together, and were proud of each other -- just like all good families. Although so many of us know Cal Ripken, Jr. as the "Iron Man," he is still a regular guy. Still a dad, a husband, and a son – all of those things.

Coming home from the airport one night, there was a mix-up. Cal didn't have a ride so I offered to take him home. We pulled up to his gate and he said, "Hit the button." His children answered, and I sat there and listened to him talk to Rachel and Ryan for about five minutes. Finally he said, "Okay, Daddy wants to get in." I drove him up to the house and said, "See ya later, Rip." For a couple of minutes I had the privilege of seeing a small piece of Cal's life that I had never seen before, and will probably never see again. It was a great night to lean back and enjoy something very ordinary and something very special at the same time.

Cal, Jr. has carried on the standards set by his parents and cultivated solid relationships with his own kids.

These same ideals had a lot to do with the very beginnings of the beliefs and ethics that are now associated with the "Oriole Way." The ballclub in Baltimore has done a good job of seeing that these standards have been carried on through the years. Brooks and Boog and Frank Robinson and Blair, and all of those outstanding players, they all came through the same organization in the same way.

The Orioles, over the years have been really blessed with an outstanding bunch of people. I'm not sure, but it may start in training camp. Maybe it begins in the minor leagues. When considering all of their success, it sure seems to be the right way to run a baseball club. Of course, there have been snags. But then again, they pick themselves up and go get the players they need to do it well.

I think more than anything else the Orioles want to cultivate those rare individuals and bring them up through their system rather than trade for players who come from varying standards and structures. There are a lot of people that exist behind the scenes that help run the Orioles organization. And they've been doing a wonderful job for many years. Their minor leagues are very well taken care of and the young guys come right up from the bottom into the demands of the Majors.

Pressure makes diamonds. Pivotal situations create clutch situations. The Ripken family knows all about rising to the occasion. Every time you come up to the plate it's a clutch situation. Every time a pitcher makes a pitch - that's a clutch situation. It's part of your life on and off of the field. You just have to learn how to handle it.

Imagine for a moment, a lifetime of clutch situations, played in thousands of consecutive games. Cal Ripken, Jr. was there every night - day after day. Good nights, bad nights. He is the epitome of a professional, much like some of the "Greats" who may have influenced him as he was coming up, Brooks Robinson, Johnny Unitas, Artie Donovan, Mike Flanagan, and Jim Palmer. All of these men not only have the God-given gift of physical ability, but they were mentally formidable, as well. And because of their charisma and integrity their relationship with the Baltimore community has endured through the years.

Much like these guys, Cal, Jr. wore orange and black particularly well. The pride he took in representing Baltimore has lasted over the years and I consider Cal to be an excellent example of the perpetuity of the Orioles tradition. All of my life I have heard certain special players referred to as real "pros." And I can't think of someone who greater exemplifies that term in baseball than Cal Ripken, Jr.

He understands the demands of being a professional athlete and generously embraces his role as a model in the community. Cal has old fashioned values and uncommon standards. He respects the people who pay their money to come and see the ballgames. On the road, Cal would go to the field to warm up and take time to sign autographs for fans. He felt that if they were good enough to come to the ballpark and wait for an autograph, he wanted to get to as many of them as he could.

He has always gained respect by giving respect.

You know that old saying, "Birds of a feather flock together?" Cal gravitated toward the same kind of guys, the ones that understood the importance of playing good ball and appreciating the fans. Maybe that's why Cal and Eddie Murray were such good friends.

These two Orioles legends are a lot alike. They are family men. They are not showboats. They don't scream and holler at people. They realize that the umpire can have a bad day just as well as we all can.

They are silent people. When they talk, listen. Because they are men of few words.

When I think about Cal, things that come to my mind include good friends, good times, and fighting the good fight. I think we would all like to look back on our own lives that way. Many of the great ones do.

The last thing that comes to my mind about Cal Ripken, Jr. is that we will never see a player like him again. We may never find another athlete that will play as well, for as long. Look at what Cal has accomplished; how many years, how many games? I've never seen anybody like him.

It takes a man with a very solid mental attitude to do it for as long as he's done it. I'm not sure how one acquires that kind of fortitude - maybe you're born with it. I don't think so. I think it is something that an athlete has got to manufacture within himself.

Some days, mentally you're right there but you have an ache or a pain. Other days you don't have an ache or a pain but you can't remember your own name. It's a demanding game - Baseball - and it's the greatest game ever played! All of us in Baltimore have been very fortunate through the years that some of the greatest athletes of all time have worn the Orioles uniform. But there will never be another Cal Ripken, Jr.

Baseball is so much fun to watch because it's such a great game. The difference between an out and a base hit is just a step. Some guys get there and some guys don't. Cal got there.

Chuck Thompson
Hall of Fame Broadcaster

Cal,
It was the highlight of my career to watch and play beside you. You are truly a hall-of-famer and represent all that is great about the game of baseball. I only wish I had the mental fortitude and dedication that you have to meet the challenge that this game presents.
Jeff Ballard

I first saw Cal in 1973 in the Southern League city of Asheville, NC. He bat boyed for his Dad's double A team. He could play then, too.
Tom Trebelhorn

"PERSEVERANCE" — THE SECRET OF ALL CAL'S TRIUMPHS
Jimmy Williams

Junior,
Congrats on a great career. But remember, don't mess with me on the floor hockey court.
Jo Nepal "The Whammer"

It was an honor to be your teammate. And a pleasure to know you personally. Hope life after baseball treats you as good as when you played. Congratulations
53
Anderson Rickey Jr.

Cal —
It has been a honor to know you as a teammate + friend. May your post baseball life bring you + your family happiness + fulfillment
signature

Hi, Cal:
Thanks for exemplifying what can be accomplished with desire and hard work, utilizing your ability and excellent skills required in our profession. You have been an inspiration and example to all ages in all walks of life. Continued success in your future endeavors. Fellow Oriole
Don Buford

Cal,
From Bluefield to Baltimore it's been great playing with you and now watching you reach such high levels of excellence. Best wishes always,
Larry Sheets

Cal
Thank you for being a true leader for all
Jeffrey Hammonds

Cal,
Our sincere congratulations on a spectacular career and many thanks for being "who you were" and "where you were" at a time, when the game of baseball "needed" you the most.
signature & Fam.

Cal Ripken is a great athlete, a great sportsman and a great Marylander. Cal's career has been marked by outstanding achievements on and off the field. He is both a complete ballplayer and a complete person.

His consecutive game streak may be the one baseball record that will never be broken. He is one of only seven players to have more than 400 home runs and 3000 hits. These accomplishments, plus appearing in 18 All-Star Games and winning the Rookie of the Year, MVP and Gold Glove honors, undoubtedly qualify him for the Baseball Hall of Fame.

Cal's remarkable record-setting statistics as a player are only part of his astonishing story. His work ethic, his constant striving for excellence, and his many contributions back to the community have established him as a role model for players and fans alike.

The Orioles are proud that he has been an integral, essential part of our team for more than two decades. He will always be a special legacy to the Orioles and our fans.

Cal Ripken has shown he loves the game of baseball, but I speak for many when I say that baseball loves him as well.

Chairman
The Baltimore Orioles

VI TAKES IN A GAME WITH CAL AND FRED
DURING THE EARLY 1960'S.

CAL JR. RECEIVED AN EARLY INTRODUCTION TO PROFESSIONAL BASEBALL AS HIS FATHER MANAGED IN THE MINORS FROM 1961-1974. HERE, THE RIPKEN CHILDREN (BOTTOM L-R: CAL, FRED, BILLY, AND ELLIE) JOIN DAD FOR FAMILY DAY IN TRI-CITY, WASHINGTON DURING THE 1965 SEASON.

ON AUGUST 24, 1960, CALVIN AND VIOLET RIPKEN BROUGHT THEIR SECOND CHILD INTO THE WORLD - A BOY THAT WAS BORN TO PLAY. AS THE SON OF A LIFELONG BASE-BALL MAN, CAL RIPKEN, JR. SPENT MUCH OF HIS CHILDHOOD AROUND THE GAME. WHILE HIS FATHER MANAGED IN RURAL AMERICAN TOWNS SUCH AS TRI-CITY AND ASHEVILLE, JUNIOR OFTEN FOLLOWED ALONG. SOMETIMES, CAL WOULD GO TO THESE MINOR LEAGUE STADIUMS TO SPEND TIME WITH HIS DAD. SHAGGING FLY BALLS, WORKING ON HIS SWING, AND HANGING AROUND A PROFESSIONAL CLUBHOUSE GAVE THE YOUNGSTER AN EARLY - AND STRONG - FOUNDATION IN THE GAME. YET, ABOVE ALL, BASEBALL WAS IN HIS BLOOD. CAL RIPKEN SR. CAUGHT SEVEN SEASONS IN THE MINORS BEFORE BECOMING A MINOR LEAGUE MANAGER, CAL FOLLOWED HIS FATHER'S PATH AND FOUND HIS INHERITED GIFT. JUNIOR DIDN'T PUR-SUE ANY OTHER AVENUE. HE LISTENED TO HIS FATHER'S INSIGHTS ON THE GAME. HE BEGAN TO UNDERSTAND THE "RIPKEN WAY."

As a Little Leaguer, Cal (second row, center) didn't play just shortstop or third base - frequently, he would be the team's catcher.

11

THE MAN OF MANY
BATTING STANCES
OFTEN RELIED ON
A PITCHING WINDUP
DURING HIS HIGH
SCHOOL YEARS.
AS A SENIOR AT
ABERDEEN (MD)
HIGH SCHOOL,
RIPKEN POSTED
A 7-2 RECORD, A
0.70 ERA AND 100
STRIKEOUTS IN
JUST 60 INNINGS.
IN 1978'S
AMATEUR DRAFT,
THE ORIOLES
WOULD SELECT HIM
AS A PITCHER.

SEATED IN THE CENTER, CAL RIPKEN, JR. JOINS HIS BUDDIES ON THE ABERDEEN BASEBALL SQUAD FOR A TEAM PICTURE. AS A HIGH SCHOOL PLAYER, YOUNG CAL WORE #7, LIKE HIS FATHER. ANOTHER PLAYER HAD HIS NOW FAMILIAR #8.

"EVEN BACK THEN, CAL WAS A VERY GOAL-ORIENTED PLAYER. HE WAS VERY DEDICATED TO HIS SPORT AND HAD A GREAT WORK ETHIC."

"REALLY, IT WAS LIKE YOU HAD ANOTHER COACH ON THE FIELD. CAL HAD A GREAT SENSE OF AWARENESS AND NEVER NEEDED TO BE REMINDED OF THE SITUATION."

-GEORGE CONNOLLY
ABERDEEN VARSITY
BASEBALL COACH

13

CAL ADVANCED TO TRIPLE-A ROCHESTER FOR THE 1981 SEASON. DURING HIS FOUR MONTHS WITH THE RED WINGS, RIPKEN PLAYED 85 GAMES AT THIRD BASE AND 35 AT SHORTSTOP.

EVEN THOUGH HE SPENT
A QUARTER OF THE
SEASON IN BALTIMORE,
RIPKEN STILL
CAPTURED THE 1981
TRIPLE-A
INTERNATIONAL
LEAGUE ROOKIE OF
THE YEAR AWARD.

17

RIPKEN PAUSES FOR HIS OFFICIAL 1982 PLAYER HEADSHOT.

CAL MANAGES TO
FIND TIME FOR A
BREAK ON THE
BENCH DURING HIS
1982 ROOKIE YEAR.

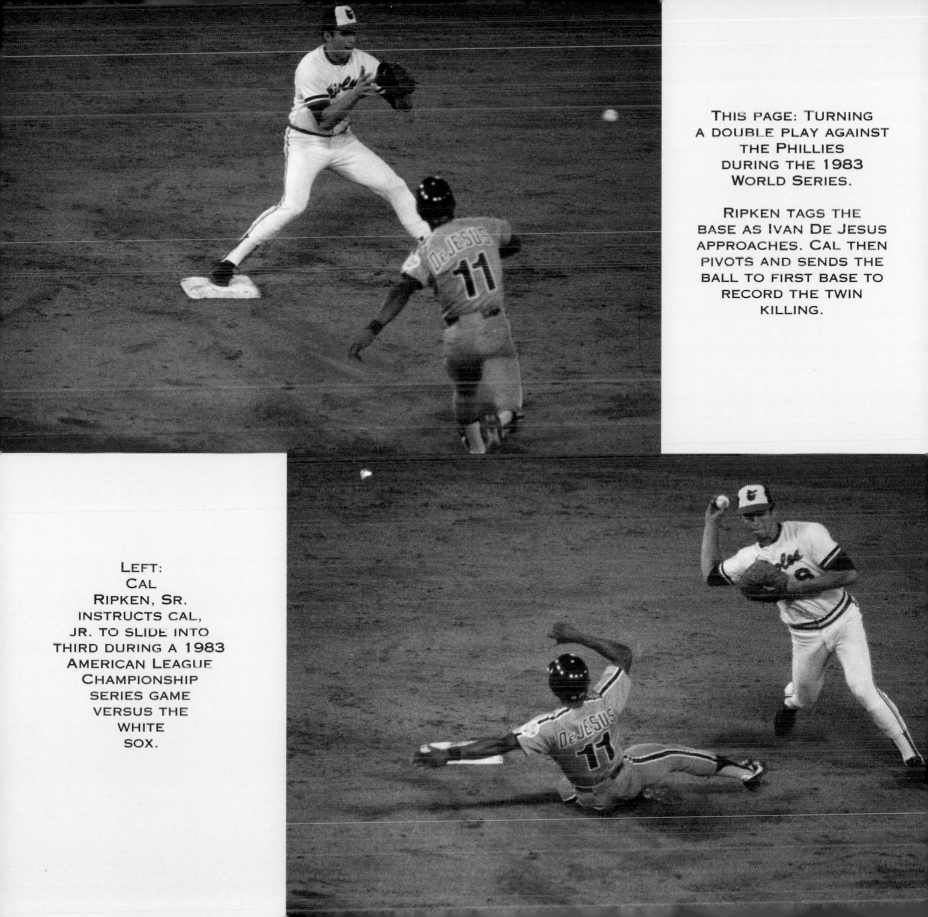

This page: Turning a double play against the Phillies during the 1983 World Series.

Ripken tags the base as Ivan De Jesus approaches. Cal then pivots and sends the ball to first base to record the twin killing.

Left: Cal Ripken, Sr. instructs Cal, Jr. to slide into third during a 1983 American League Championship series game versus the White Sox.

Even a high pop-up in the sun couldn't keep this defensive great down. After averaging 22 errors per year in the early 80's, Ripken's defense would improve with age. Throughout the first half of the 1990's, single-digit season error totals became the norm.

CAL, SR. AND JR. SPENT ELEVEN YEARS TOGETHER ON 33RD STREET. IT WAS IN THIS HOUSE OF MAGIC THAT CAL RIPKEN, JR. BLOSSOMED INTO A MAJOR LEAGUE SUPERSTAR AND WHERE CAL, SR. COACHED, MANAGED, THEN COACHED AGAIN UNTIL THE GRAND OLD LADY CLOSED HER DOORS ON OCTOBER 6, 1991.

IN THE END, IT WAS CAL, JR. WHO TOOK THE LAST SWING AT MEMORIAL STADIUM.

24

ON "GLOVE DAY" AT MEMORIAL STADIUM -
AND EVERY DAY - ORIOLES FANS LOVE CAL.

27

PROCEEDING PAGES:

AT THE PLATE IN 1984.

"ON THE READY" IN 1982.

The Orioles superstars of the 1980's - Eddie Murray and Cal Ripken, Jr.

RIPKEN HOLDS HIS GROUND AND MAKES
THE TAG VERSUS MILWAUKEE IN 1990.

33

DESPITE THE ALL-OUT EFFORT OF RED SOX STAR WADE BOGGS,
RIPKEN PULLS OFF THIS DOUBLE PLAY IN 1991 AT MEMORIAL STADIUM.

QUICK GROUNDER TO SHORT...RIPKEN MAKES
A DIVE TO HIS LEFT AND FROM HIS KNEES
MAKES THE THROW TO FIRST.

AFTER GETTING DOWN AND DIRTY, CAL
WATCHES THE BALL SAIL ACROSS THE
INFIELD TO FINISH OFF A SPECTACULAR PLAY.

37

A RETURN TO THE HOT CORNER:
CAL PLAYS THE 1997 SEASON AS THE
ORIOLES' EVERYDAY THIRD BASEMAN.

THE IRONMAN

PREPARING TO
SQUARE OFF DURING
ORIOLE PARK'S 1993
ALL-STAR SEASON.

42

Cal, Sr.

CAL RIPKEN, SR. SPENT 36 SEASONS IN THE BALTIMORE ORIOLES ORGANIZATION. OVER THE COURSE OF HIS CAREER, HE CRAFTED COUNTLESS YOUNG PLAYERS INTO FINE ATHLETES AND MODELS OF THE "ORIOLE WAY" - INCLUDING HIS SONS.

CAL RIPKEN, SR. SPENT EACH DAY
AS BOTH A TEACHER AND A DIRECTOR.
BEFORE GAMES, SENIOR WOULD HIT
COUNTLESS FUNGOES AND PITCHED
BP WITH A CATCHER'S MITT.

THE ELDER RIPKEN ALWAYS VOICED
HIS BELIEF THAT "PRACTICE DOESN'T
MAKE PERFECT - PERFECT
PRACTICE MAKES PERFECT."

IN THE THIRD BASE COACH'S
BOX, HE WOULD FLASH
SIGNALS TO ORIOLES HITTERS
AND BASERUNNERS - AND
WHEN THEIR WORK PAID OFF,
HE ACKNOWLEDGED
THEIR EFFORTS.

HERE, SENIOR OFFERS A
HANDSHAKE AND PAT ON
THE BACK TO CAL, JR.
AFTER A HOME RUN
IN 1991.

Father and son greet fans with Orioles calendars during the 1991 final weekend at Memorial Stadium.

On the field and in the clubhouse, Junior simply called his father, "Senior."

1992: ORIOLES TOGETHER FOR THE FINAL TIME.

FROM 1987 TO 1992, THE RIPKEN BOYS PLAYED SIDE-BY-SIDE IN THE INFIELD OF THEIR HOMETOWN TEAM. IN '96, BILLY RETURNED TO BALTIMORE FOR ONE MORE SEASON TO BACK UP ALL-STAR SECOND BASEMAN ROBERTO ALOMAR.

1987

AS BASEBALL PLAYERS – AND AS PEOPLE – CAL AND BILLY WERE OFTEN VIEWED AS COMPLETE OPPOSITES. CAL BLASTED HOMERS. BILLY BLOOPED SINGLES.

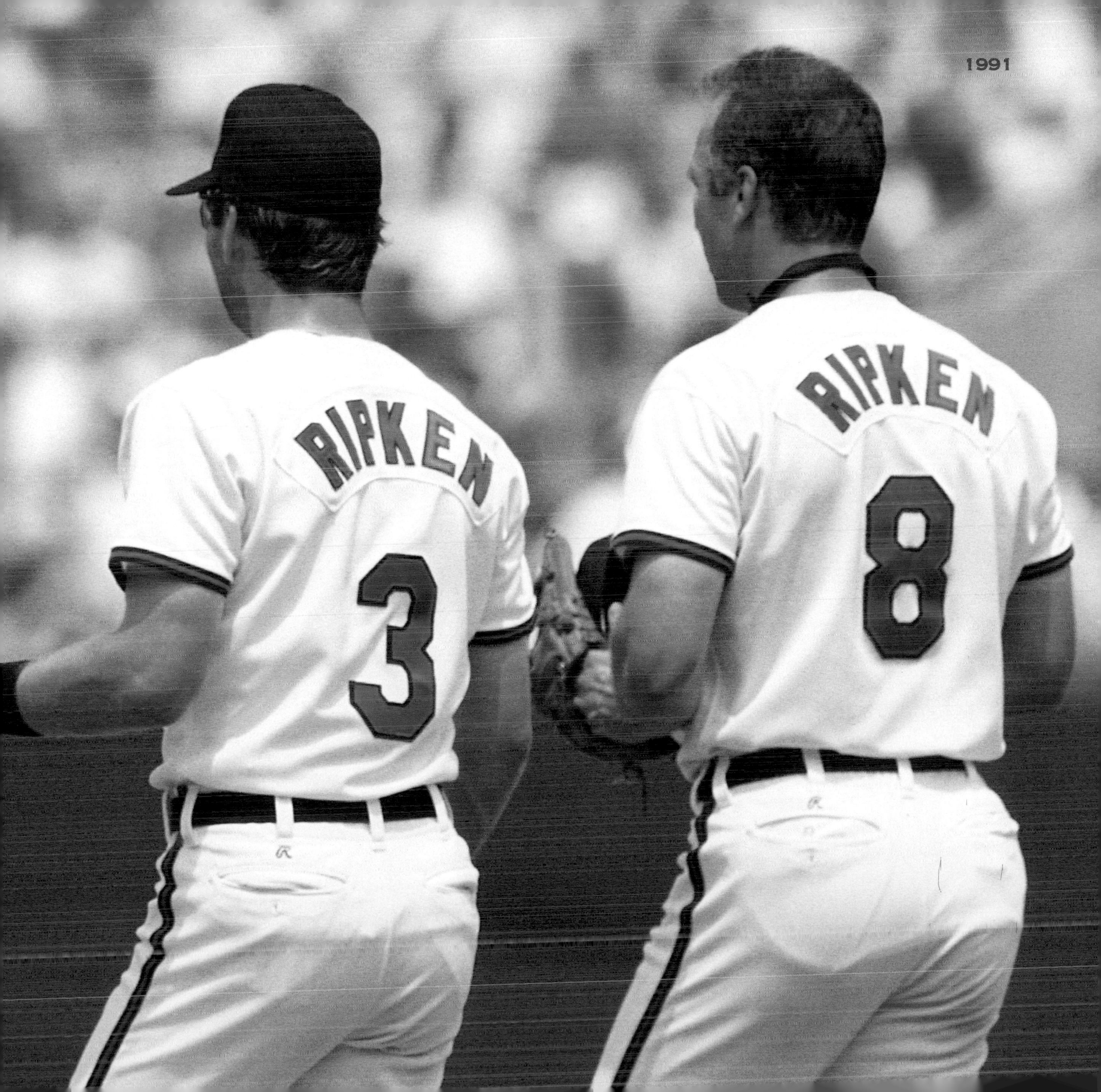

1991

CAL AND HIS SON, RYAN
DURING THE 2131 FIFTH INNING
CELEBRATION ON SEPTEMBER 6, 1995.

2,130+
HUGS AND KISSES
FOR DADDY

THE RIPKENS ON ORIOLES FAMILY DAY 1999. LEFT TO RIGHT: KELLY, RACHEL, CAL, AND RYAN.

CAL AND VI TOGETHER ON SEPTEMBER 2, 1999.

FOLLOWING CAL RIPKEN, SR.'S PASSING, THE ORIOLES HONORED HIS MEMORY BY PLACING HIS JERSEY NUMBER ON THE OFFICIAL UNIFORM FOR THE ENTIRE 1999 SEASON. IT INCLUDED THIS NIGHT WHEN RIPKEN HIT CAREER HOME RUN #400.

team

64

CAL AND EDDIE MURRAY WERE ONCE THE HEART AND SOUL OF THE BALTIMORE ORIOLES.
SOON, THEY WILL BE TEAMMATES AGAIN - HALL OF FAMERS IN COOPERSTOWN, NEW YORK.

65

fans

History will look fondly upon Cal Ripken, Jr. for much more than baseball records and statistics. Fans do love and admire his athleticism and perseverance. But it's really his hard work ethic, his pursuit of excellence, and his relationship with the Baltimore community that will ultimately leave their mark on time.

Over the years, Ripken has given much back to his hometown. Cal's efforts are centered around literacy and youth baseball initiatives.

Recently, Cal has become closer than ever to young baseball players. His goal is to bring the element of fun back to the sandlot. He hopes to pass on the joy of America's Pastime to kids, parents and coaches.

In 2002, Ripken's "Aberdeen Project" will be complete, and a one-of-a-kind international baseball complex will open in the Iron Man's hometown. This youth baseball academy will house a 6,500 seat minor league stadium and a number of little-league sized fields, including ones modeled after Oriole Park, Memorial Stadium and Wrigley Field.

Even though Cal Ripken, Jr. decided that the 2001 season would be his last, his contributions to the community and the game of baseball will continue on.

CAL,
I've waited
my whole life
to see
YOU!!

72

TOP LEFT: CAL GIVES LOTS OF HIS TIME TO KIDS IN THE COMMUNITY.

TOP RIGHT: 1991 GOVERNOR'S PROCLAMATION.

BOTTOM LEFT: SPENDING TIME WITH HIS YOUNG FANS.

BOTTOM RIGHT: FAN APPRECIATION WEEK 2000 .

1982	A.L Rookie of the Year
1983	American League MVP World ChampionSHIP
1984	Hits for the Cycle
1987	Consecutive Innings streak ends at 8,243
1990	95 straight errorless games
1991	All-Star Home Run Derby champion All-Star Game MVP Gold Glove winner American League MVP
1992	Gold Glove winner
1993	Sets Shortstop Home Run Record
1995	Breaks Lou Gehrig's streak with 2131
1996	Streak sets World Record at 2216
1998	The Streak ends, etching "2632" into history
1999	400th Home Run
2000	3,000th Hit
2001	All-Star Game MVP

75

legendary accomplishments

CAL RIPKEN, JR. BEGAN 1982 - HIS FIRST FULL BIG LEAGUE SEASON - ON OPENING DAY WITH A MAJOR LEAGUE HOME RUN.

HE ENDED THAT INAUGURAL CAMPAIGN BY CAPTURING THE AMERICAN LEAGUE'S ROOKIE OF THE YEAR AWARD.

RIPKEN LED ALL 1982 ROOKIES IN DOUBLES, HOMERS, RBI, TOTAL BASES, GAMES AND RUNS. IN VOTING FOR THE A.L. ROY, CAL'S 132 VOTES OUTNUMBERED MINNESOTA'S KENT HRBEK (90 POINTS) AND BOSTON'S WADE BOGGS (10.5). EVERY SINGLE BALLOT INCLUDED RIPKEN'S NAME.

THANKS TO HIS BREAKTHROUGH .264, 28 HR, 93 RBI YEAR, RIPKEN JOINED RON HANSEN ('60), CURT BLEFARY ('65), AL BUMBRY ('73), AND EDDIE MURRAY ('77) AS AN ORIOLE ROOKIE OF THE YEAR RECIPIENT.

CAL RECEIVES AMERICAN LEAGUE ROOKIE OF THE YEAR PLAQUE FROM ORIOLES GENERAL MANAGER HANK PETERS.

CELEBRATING THE ORIOLES' 1983 WORLD CHAMPIONSHIP VICTORY.

1991
ALL-STAR MVP.

After being selected as a reserve in 1983, annual All-Star appearances became the norm for Ripken.

Cal's most memorable performances during the mid-summer classic came in 1991 at Toronto's SkyDome and in 2001 at Safeco Field, Seattle. After hitting home runs in each of these contests, Cal was named the game's MVP. By winning the 2001 award, the retiring legend joined Willie Mays, Steve Garvey and Gary Carter as one of four players to be named All-Star Game MVP twice.

2-Time American League MVP

Ripken followed up his 1982 Rookie of the Year season with an A.L. MVP winning campaign in 1983. In the process, Cal became the first to win Rookie and MVP honors in successive years. Ripken captured the prize by beating out teammate Eddie Murray, 322-290, in balloting. Eight seasons later (1991), Cal posted even better numbers, and was awarded another American League MVP beating out Detroit slugger Cecil Fielder.

Brooks Robinson, Frank Robinson and Boog Powell are the other Orioles who have won an American League MVP. However, Cal Ripken, Jr. is the only Oriole to have ever been awarded two of these honors. He is one of 22 players in M.L. history to be named MVP more than once.

4-Time Most Valuable Oriole

The Louis M. Hatter Most Valuable Oriole Award is presented annually to the player whose contributions and statistics rise above and beyond those of his teammates.

Ripken was selected as the "MVO" four times in total. Twice, he was awarded the honor outright (1990 and 1991). On two other occasions, Cal shared the distinction with Eddie Murray (1983 and 1988).

The award is selected by a vote of writers and broadcasters who cover the Orioles on a regular basis.

Most Valuable Player Awards

For 21 seasons, Orioles fans witnessed the illustrious career of Cal Ripken, Jr. unfold. Over the years, Ripken gave onlookers many reasons to celebrate his achievements. From Rookie of the Year and MVP awards to reaching 400 home runs and 3000 hits, his career was always one highlight after another.

However, most would consider the pinnacle of Cal's brilliant career to what culminated into one special series six years ago against the California Angels.

During two glorious nights in September of 1995, Cal Ripken, Jr. tied - then broke - the record that was long thought to be untouchable. Ripken reached the immortal Lou Gehrig's 2,130 consecutive games mark, then etched his own name into the annals of America's greatest game.

On the field, the Angels fell to the Orioles on both September 5th (2130) and September 6th (2131). For 2130, RHP Scott Erickson blanked the Halos 8-0. The next day, as Ripken broke the record, RHP Mike Mussina led the O's to a 4-2 victory. Both nights, Cal took California pitching deep as the Baltimore baseball legend rose to the occasion with home runs.

In a career that includes so many impressive statistics and highlights, what happened on these two September nights has become the ultimate and signature moment of Cal Ripken Jr.'s career and will remain on of the most unforgettable in baseball history.

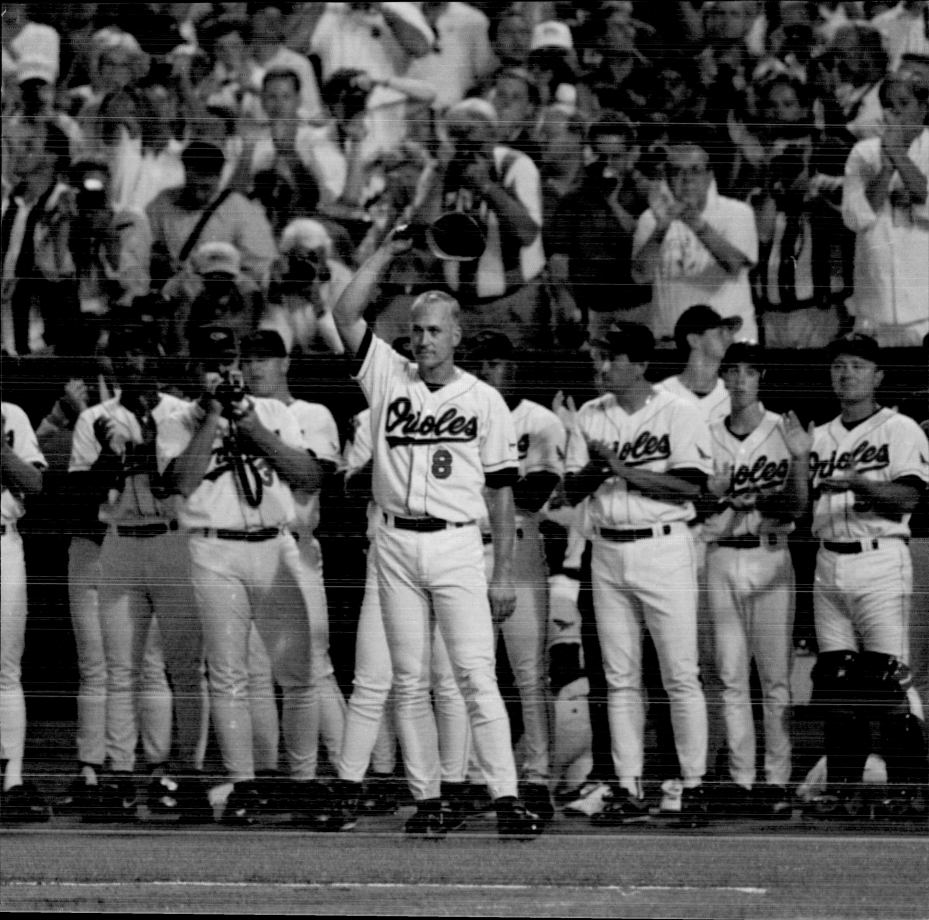

MAKING 5TH INNING CURTAIN CALLS DURING THE RECORD BREAKING GAME.

Upon breaking Lou Gehrig's consecutive games played record on September 6, 1995, Cal Ripken, Jr. continued on to make his own distinctive mark on the record books. For the next three seasons and 501 additional games, Ripken persevered, continuing to play each day without exception. The athlete, who had come to be known as the "Iron Man," fought the good fight until taking a well-deserved break from the action on September 20, 1998.

On that evening, in front of many of the same hometown fans who had watched him grow and prosper, Cal ended his streak and etched "2632" into the history books.

During Ripken's run of consecutive games that spanned from May 30, 1982 until September 19, 1998, more things changed than remained the same in the world.

Sixteen years had hurled by as Ripken, like many of us, went to work every day. During that time, three different men occupied the White House, Baltimore lost its NFL franchise - then acquired a new one, and 26 players suited up as Cal's double-play partner.

Time and tides wait for no man. Politics, local affairs, and professional sports are no exceptions. In the whole scheme of things, "The Streak" represents much more than a series of actions that have accumulated over periods of time. We could all learn from Ripken's accomplishments and longevity. These feats are testament to a great measure of moral principle and ideals.

Each one of the hundreds of players that moved through the Orioles organization during the 1980's and 1990's, knew they could rely on Cal's infield support. It left one slot in the daily lineup card as a complete certainty for the seven skippers that managed the club over this period.

The Major League Baseball season of 162 games isn't a sprint, but a marathon. Over the course of this endurance race, nagging injuries and general fatigue inevitably creep up on an athlete. Sooner or later, these distractions may erode a player's performance.

There is no doubt that Ripken suffered from his share of countless injuries and exhaustion. Living the life of a professional athlete, every day for seven months out of every

YEAR, WOULD LIKELY DO THAT TO ANYONE. YET, UNLIKE OTHER MAJOR LEAGUERS WHO TAKE TIME OFF TO NURSE A GIMPY ANKLE OR DEAL WITH THE FLU, CAL KNEW THAT HIS TEAMMATES NEEDED HIM IN THE LINEUP AND NEVER REQUESTED A DAY OFF.

SPEAKING OF CALLING IN SICK, CONSIDER THIS. DURING THE EARLY 1920'S THE NEW YORK YANKEES HAD A FINE FIRST BASEMAN NAMED WALLY PIPP, WHOSE 15-YEAR CAREER INCLUDED A .282 LIFETIME BATTING AVERAGE, NEARLY 1000 RBI, AND TWO SINGLE-SEASON HOME RUN CROWNS. IN 1925, PIPP WAS A BASEBALL STAR. HOWEVER, THE HISTORY BOOKS REMEMBER HIM FOR THE HEADACHE THAT FORCED HIM TO SIT OUT FOR ONE VERY SPECIAL GAME.

IT WAS TO BE A YOUNG LOU GEHRIG WHO WOULD TAKE HIS PLACE IN THE LINEUP. WALLY NEVER GOT HIS JOB BACK AS THE YANKEES' FIRST BASEMAN, AND GEHRIG WENT ON TO PLAY 2,130 CONSECUTIVE GAMES.

FOR ONE PIVOTAL DAY IN 1925, WALLY PIPP WASN'T AT THE TOP OF HIS GAME AND THINGS WERE NEVER TO BE THE SAME.

RIPKEN, LIKE GEHRIG BECAME KNOWN FOR HIS COMMITMENT AND PERSEVERANCE. AFTER CAPTURING THE 1983 WORLD SERIES CHAMPIONSHIP, THE FRANCHISE ENDURED SOME LEAN YEARS, INCLUDING THE 107-LOSS 1988 ORIOLES TEAM. DESPITE THE TRIALS AND TRIBULATIONS OF STRUGGLING SEASONS, RIPKEN PLAYED HARD AS IF EACH GAME COULD MAKE A DIFFERENCE.

DURING "THE STREAK" YEARS, CAL PROVED THAT HIS COMMITMENT TO THE BALLCLUB, HIS TEAMMATES, AND THE FANS WAS AS STRONG AS EVER. LOOKING BACK, ONE MIGHT SAY THAT HIS ALLEGIANCE TO BALTIMORE AND THE SANCTITY OF AMERICA'S FAVORITE PASTIME WAS HIS GREATEST ATTRIBUTE.

RIPKEN NEVER SET OUT TO BREAK A RECORD OR BECOME A HERO. HE REACHED, THEN PASSED LOU GEHRIG'S RECORD BECAUSE OF THE STANDARDS HE SET FOR HIMSELF AS AN INDIVIDUAL, AS A PROFESSIONAL, AND AS A BALTIMORE ORIOLE.

JOHN STEADMAN, LENGENDARY *BALTIMORE SUN* SPORTS WRITER, INTERVIEWED CAL IN 1992. "MY EMPHASIS HAS NEVER BEEN ON LOU'S RECORD," RIPKEN TOLD STEADMAN. "IN FACT, I DELIBERATE-LY TRY TO KEEP GEHRIG AND THE RECORD OUT OF MY THINKING. PLAYING EVERY DAY IS A MATTER OF PERSONAL PRIDE. I STARTED MY CAREER WITH THE THOUGHT OF BEING INVOLVED IN THE GAME EVERY DAY TO HELP THE ORIOLES WIN. I APPRECIATE THE RECOGNITION I HAVE GOTTEN FOR BEING A GOOD CITIZEN."

92

Cal Ripken, Jr. never recorded 40 home runs in a season. He was to reach 30 homers only once during his 21 years in the Major League (34 in 1991).

17 years after his first career home run, Ripken notched #400 on September 2, 1999 at Oriole Park at Camden Yards. His shot off Devil Rays' starting pitcher Rolando Arrojo made him the 29th player in Major League history to join the 400 Home Run Club.

While former baseball greats like Al Kaline and Dale Murphy finished just inches short of the mark before retiring, Ripken met the milestone, and made another impression upon baseball history.

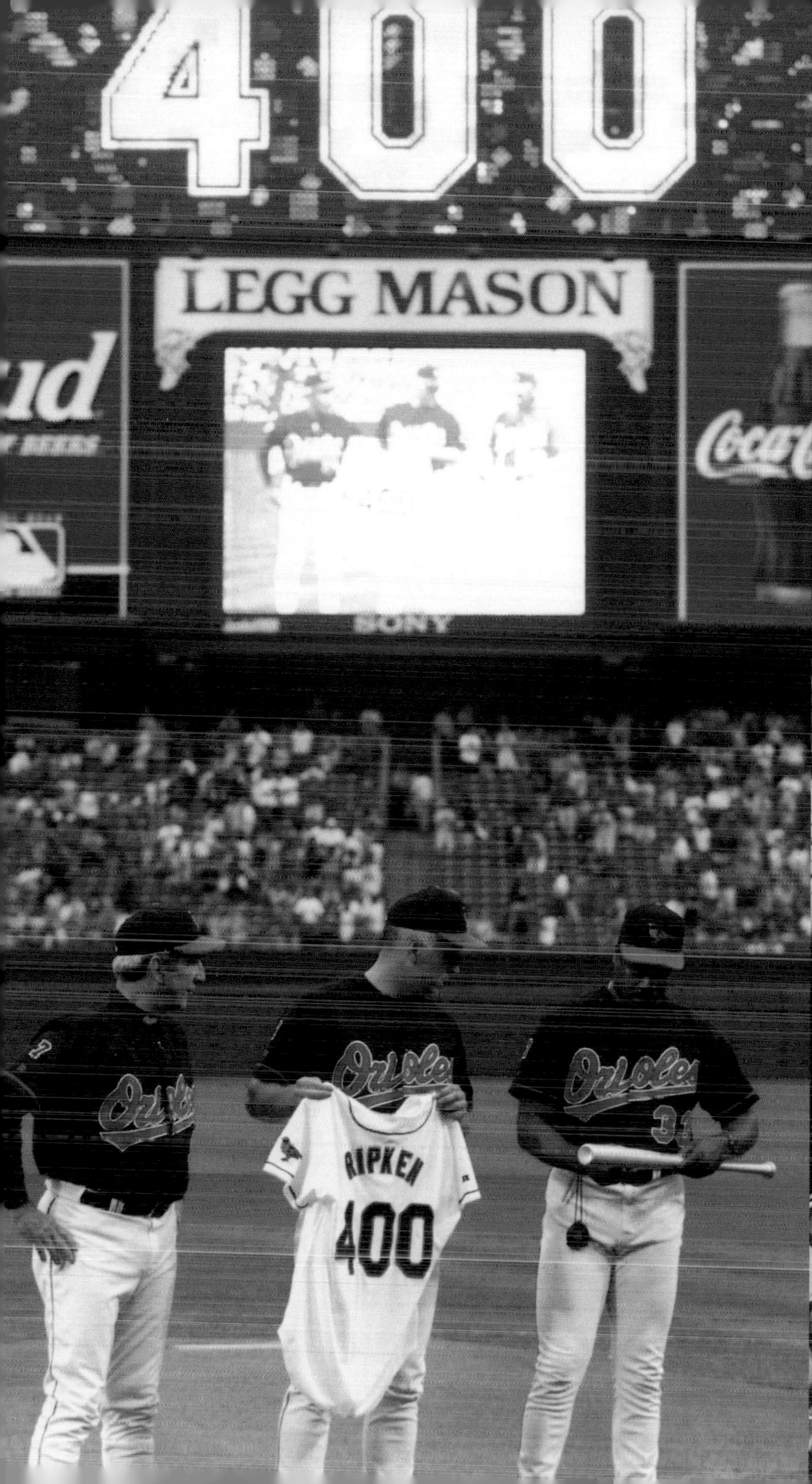
400
LEGG MASON
SONY
RIPKEN
400

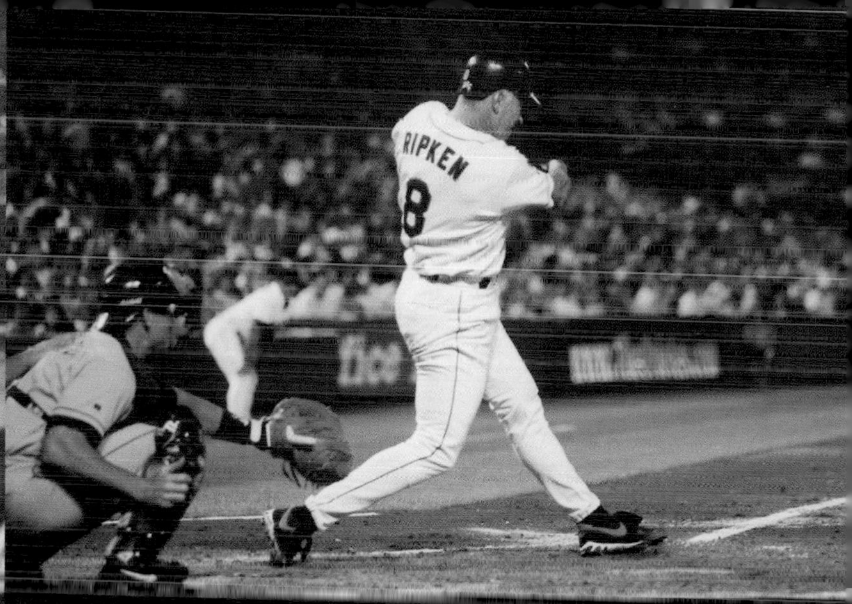
RIPKEN
8

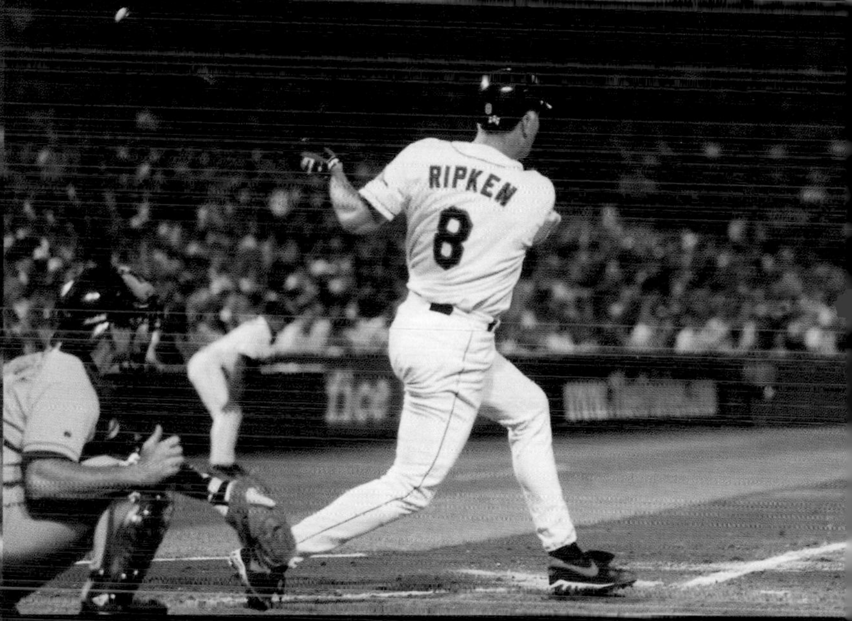
RIPKEN
8

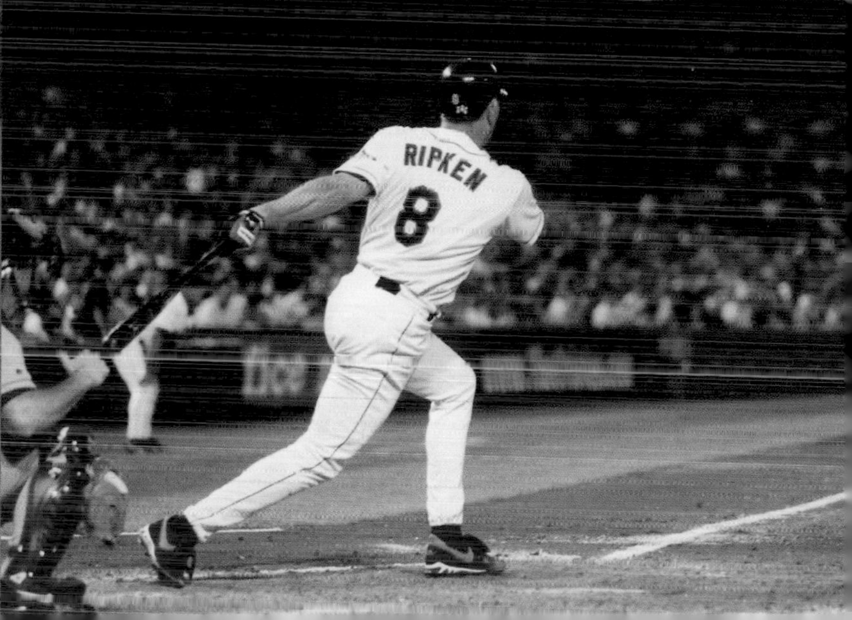
RIPKEN
8

BASEBALL IS A GAME OF STATISTICS, NUMBERS AND CAREER ACHIEVEMENTS. FROM THE 300-WIN MARK FOR PITCHERS, TO 500 HOME RUNS, AND ON TO 3,000 HITS, THESE ARE THE MAGICAL NUMBERS OF AMERICA'S PASTIME. A PLAYER CANNOT REACH THESE LEVELS OF BASEBALL IMMORTALITY BY SIMPLY BEING GOOD - OR EVEN BY BEING OUTSTANDING - IN THE SHORT RUN.

REACHING THE 3,000 HIT CLUB IS AN IMPROBABLE TASK IF YOU CAN'T PLAY AT A HIGH LEVEL AND DO SO FOR AN EXTENDED PERIOD OF TIME.

THE REALITY OF 3,000 HITS IS TRULY AWE INSPIRING. IT IS A MILESTONE THAT ONLY 23 OTHER MAJOR LEAGUERS HAVE EVER REACHED. IT IS A LANDMARK FIGURE THAT LEADS TO A REALIZATION OF GREATNESS AND GIVES WAY TO THRILLING CELEBRATIONS.

CAL'S JOURNEY TO 3,000 BEGAN ON AUGUST 16, 1981 WHEN HE KNOCKED A SINGLE OFF WHITE SOX HURLER DENNIS LAMP. IN THE YEARS SINCE, RIPKEN'S DEPENDABLE NATURE TYPICALLY PROVIDED HIS TEAM WITH AT LEAST 150 HITS PER SEASON.

95

CAL SINGLES OFF TWINS PITCHER HECTOR CARRASCO ON APRIL 15, 2000 AT THE METRODOME FOR CAREER HIT #3000.

THE TWO RETIRING LEGENDS OF 2001 – TONY GWYNN AND CAL RIPKEN, JR. POSE FOR PHOTOS BEFORE THEIR FINAL ALL-STAR GAME.

LIKE FATHER, LIKE SON:
CAL RIPKEN, JR. AND
SON, RYAN AT THE
2001 ALL-STAR GAME.

LEFT: EVEN AFTER SURPASSING GEHRIG'S RECORD ON SEPTEMBER 6, 1995, RIPKEN STILL DID NOT OWN THE WORLD RECORD OF 2,215 STRAIGHT GAMES HELD BY JAPAN'S SACHIO KINUGASA.

CAL BEAT THAT MARK ON JUNE 14, 1996 IN KANSAS CITY AND HAD THE CHANCE TO MEET AND TALK WITH THE JAPANESE BASEBALL LEGEND.

BELOW: TWO WEEKS AFTER REACHING THE 3,000 HIT PLATEAU, THE ORIOLES HONORED RIPKEN AT CAMDEN YARDS WITH A WONDERFUL PRE-GAME TRIBUTE. WITH THE NUMBER "3000" ON THE WAREHOUSE, HIT CLUB MEMBERS EDDIE MURRAY AND DAVE WINFIELD (PICTURED) TOOK THE MICROPHONE TO OFFER THEIR CONGRATULATIONS.

TOP LEFT
RECEIVING ONE OF HIS EIGH
SILVER SLUGGER AWARDS

TOP RIGHT
RIPKEN HOLDS AN ESPY O
HIS OWN AT THE FEBRUAR
1996 AWARDS SHOW

BOTTOM LEFT
WITH SON, RYAN LOOKIN
ON, BASEBAL
COMMISSIONER BUD SEL
PRESENTS CAL WITH H
2001 ALL-STAR MVP AWARE

BOTTOM RIGHT
ERNIE BANK
CONGRATULATES CAL FO
BREAKING HIS SHORTSTO
HOME RUN RECORD IN 199

"It's been a great run. Looking back, my career has gone by pretty fast.
I don't see this as an ending. I'm just moving on."
– Cal Ripken, Jr. announcing his retirement on June 19, 2001.

CAL RIPKEN IS THE ULTIMATE PROFESSIONAL! HE IS ONE OF THE TRUE ICONS OF THE GAME AND WILL TRULY BE MISSED!

CJ Bo

Cal —
Thanks for being true to your profession, to playing the game the way it was meant to be played by those who truly love it, and who proved it every time he set foot on a playing field. It has been a privilege to watch you and to ___

Hank Peters

Cal,
You have come from Aberdeen, Maryland to become a world wide personality. All along the way you have been the model of class and dignity. Throw in what you have done all of these years on the field and it adds up to something very special.
Best always,
The Skipper

It has been an honor to play with a legend like you Cal and just watching you work and play the game the way you do has helped me a lot in the 3 years I have been here with the Orioles.
Thanks for Everything,
Jason Johnson

I have had the opportunity to play with Cal and without question he is and was a true student of the game. Many young up and coming players may often emulate but will never duplicate him. Thanks for being a teammate and friend.
#43

Cal,
All of us in baseball share a little of each other in some way; your mark is simply greater than most. I hope I have left a small part of myself with you.
This is no farewell.... It will be exciting to watch your contributions continue.
Way to Go! *Sam Perlozzo*

Rip,
"The ultimate gamer." I enjoyed every moment we played together. Thanks for everything!

Jeff Robolt

I have been around some great athletes in my time. But I have never been around one that has given as much back to the game anymore

Mike Flanagan

CAL, ENJOYED OUR PLAYING DAYS TOGETHER IN B-MORE. YOUR DAD WAS ONE OF MY FAVORITE BASEBALL PEOPLE. CONGRATS ON A GREAT CAREER. THE GAMES PLAYED RECORD IS OK, BUT I AM RATHER IMPRESSED BY THE BATTING STANCES WHICH CAME WITH EACH GAME. NOW FOR THE REAL WORLD AND ... GOLF. THAT WILL BE YOUR BIGGEST CHALLENGE. ALL THE BEST TO YOU AND YOUR FAMILY

Fred Lynn

Cal,
I will never forget the last out in 83'. What a special time that was. You are a tribute to the game

Scott McGregor

To Cal,
Congrats on an awesome career!! Nobody did it Better!! Your Friend!

#31

CAL HAS THE BEST SPECIFIC PRECISE PRE MAME PREPARATION PLAN I HAVE EVER WITNESSED. THIS IS THE PRIMARY REASON FN HIS PROFESSIONAL STELLAR MOOR LEAGUE CAREER

Cal,
Over the past 20 plus years I have watched you. The work ethic, the determination, the leadership, and the pride, you display day in and day out has made me proud to be associated with you. Thank you for allowing me to be a small part of a magnificent career. I will miss you

Elvie Hendricks

Cal —
Good Luck on your Retirement. You have been a great Example for baseball in your Career - It was an honor to be your manager — *Phil Regan*

Everyone will remember the player. I will remember the man Cal-a belated thanks for making a fortunate newcomer feel so welcome during the '83 World Series run. All the best.
Tito Landrum

RIP,
FROM BLUEFIELD TO BALTIMORE YOU'VE BEEN THE BEST. THIS SMALL SPACE IS NOT ENOUGH TO TELL YOU WHAT YOU'VE MEANT TO ME AS A FRIEND AND A TEAMMATE. CONGRADULATIONS, AND WE'LL SEE YOU IN THE HALL. YOUR OLD ROOMIE
BOB

Calbo,
Just want to wish you well in your endeavors after baseball. It has been a pleasure playing with you over the years. You've been a true inspiration to a lot of people. Don't ever change!
Mussy

farewell.